A 44 mm cork wine stopper contains almost 800 million cells and each one is, in effect, a suction cup.

CORK & WINE

William A. Preston

Illuminations Press
St. Helena, California 94574

Library of Congress Catalog Number:82-084428
ISBN 0-937088-04-8

Contents

Introduction

Now the wine is mature. Year after year after year complex chemical processes have taken place protected against interference from the outside world. Nothing has entered the bottle, nothing has left it. The closure has done its work. It is made of cork - a natural material.

Cork is the most widely used closure material in the industry. There are good reasons for this. Tradition and availability play a big part, of course. Cork has been used as a wine closure since glass bottles appeared some two and a half centuries ago. The material has performed well and it is readily available. And it will continue to be available; of the twenty billion cork stoppers produced in 1980, less than three percent were shipped to United States wineries. The premium wine industry in the United States is experiencing phenomenal growth but it must multiply itself many, many times before the supply of cork would become inadequate.

A rapidly growing industry needs to accelerate its productivity. This stimulates technology, new processes, and new machines and new ideas emerge. Wine production expands and marketing creates innovative merchandising and selling techniques. New packaging methods and materials are developed and promoted. Changing technologies also create information gaps. Misunderstandings are generated and compounded. The nature and the capabilities of the cork industry and its application to the wine industry have become subject to widespread misconceptions. We hope to put to rest some of the prevailing myths and misunderstandings with this book.

To do this, the basic questions need to be answered. Why cork — what are its characteristics? What are the requirements of an effective wine closure? What is the cork

industry and what are the processes that produce wine closures? What are the production requirements for wine closures in the modern winery?

While we are concerned principally with cork, we will explore alternative methods of closure for wines and examine their performance relative to the traditional cork closure. Indeed, there are alternative materials and ways for achieving the desired results and these need to be analyzed and evaluated.

My interest in cork has developed during the last ten years because of my responsibilities as chief executive officer of APM, Inc. in Benicia, California. In that time, APM has evolved into the principal supplier of corks and stoppers to the wine industry. Early on, I became fascinated and frustrated by the widespread misconceptions about cork and its practicality and availability for the industry. Hopefully, we have dealt with these. Technical work on the subject is sparse. Perhaps we can encourage more by raising the awareness level. Exciting developments are taking place in the wine industry and it is important that we keep abreast of them.

I would like to acknowledge the counsel and help of our many friends in the wine industry. They deal with the real problems every day. Many thanks, also, to the staff at APM who work every day to improve the quality of the closures supplied to the wine industry. And, most important of all, to our good friends in Portugal, I can only say, "Muito Obrigade".

Wine stoppers hermetically sealed for shipment to winery.

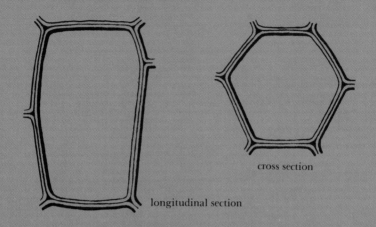

cross section

longitudinal section

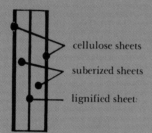

cellulose sheets

suberized sheets

lignified sheet

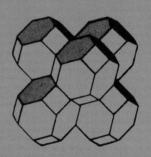

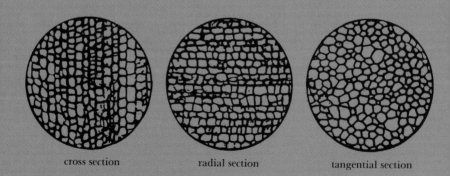

cross section

radial section

tangential section

Cork — A Unique Material

Cork is a natural vegetable tissue composed of cells with a peculiar shape, structure, and distribution, resulting in an extraordinary construction. The cells are banded together in a perfectly regular manner at a rate of about 40 million per cubic centimeter. This means a 44 mm wine cork contains almost 800 million cells and each one is, in effect, a suction cup.

Many of the unique properties of cork are due to the nature of the cellular membranes. The cells are 14-sided polyhedrons, joining together with no space between them. The membranes or walls separating the cells consist of five sheets or layers. We speak of these as sheets only for convenience of description. Given the size of the cells, these walls are actually fine threads. However, there are five layers or sheets. The two outer sheets enclosing the cavities, are made up of a cellulose substance. The central sheet is lignified, its woody quality giving the structure its rigidity. Between the central and outer layers are two layers of suberous matter, which is impermeable. Suberin is the basic substance of cork. It is the tissue which makes cork unique and gives it its particular characteristics.

The cells are filled with a mixture of gases, much like air without carbon dioxide. Almost 90% of cork's volume consists of this air-like gas filling the cell cavities.

Thus, cork consists of a fine honeycomb of five-layered sheets enclosing small spaces or cells which are filled with nitrogen and oxygen and the other gases of air without carbon dioxide. The separate layers of the cell walls are composed of materials which have different characteristics. Each plays its part in the uniqueness of cork. There is no other material, natural or manmade, which possesses all of the characteristics of cork.

Its component materials and structure give cork a unique set of physical and mechanical properties.

Lightness — Cork is very light in weight, its density ranging between .13 and .25

Impermeability —Cork is very resistant to moisture penetration. The maximum rate of water absorption is less than 18%, minimizing the threat of contamination.

Compressibility — Cork is capable of compression to half of its dimension with no loss of its flexibility. Cork is the only solid which may be compressed without the tendency to lateral extrusion.

Flexibility — Removed from compression, cork will recover about 85% of its initial volume immediately and more than 98% after 24 hours.

Adherence — The slicing of the surface cells in forming a cork stopper produces an extraordinary cupping effect. Millions of cells are opened and function as suction cups. This and the residue of suberins and waxes provide an exceptional power of adhesion to wet,smooth surfaces.

Temperature stability — Cork retains its properties at both high and low extremes of temperatures.

Age Stability — Chemically inert, resistant to insects, viruses and other micro-organisms, cork is resistant to age deterioration almost indefinitely. Twenty bottles were found in a cave in Inche-Laire, France in 1956. Dating from 1789, the beginning of the French Revolution, the cork stoppers were in perfect condition.

Cork possesses an ensemble of exclusive properties appropriate to bottling wine. It is compressible for penetrating the bottle opening. It is elastic and returns to

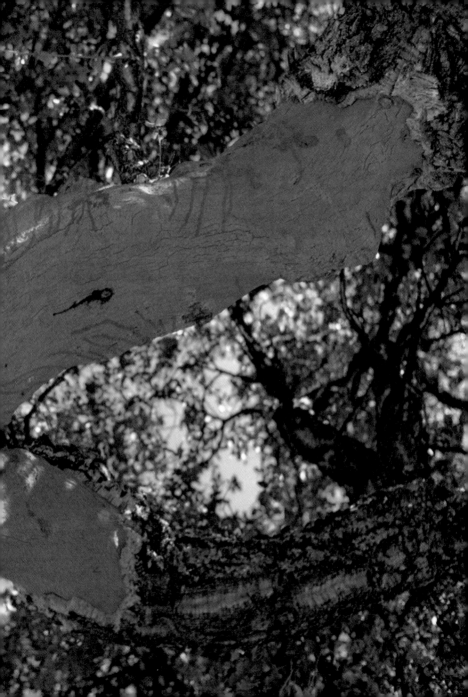

its shape to seal the opening. It has unusual adhesion to maintain the seal. It is highly resistant to contamination, through moisture or gases, and to aging. And it is truly the only material that tolerates imperfections in glass and compensates for them.

The Source

Cork is bark of a tree called the cork oak (L.-Quercus suber). Most trees will die if their bark is removed, because the bark helps to carry the sap essential to the life of the tree. The cork oak, however, has two layers of bark. The inner layer is alive and it is the base on which a new inner layer grows each year. As the old layers move outward and die, they serve as insulation, protecting the tree from the hot arid winds in the growing areas. The dead outer layer can be stripped away without injuring the tree but care must be taken not to penetrate the inner living bark. Damage to this inner layer will prevent the growth of the cork and can kill the tree.

The harvesting of the outer layer of cork follows the same pattern as the harvesting of wine grapes and every other growing product. It waits until the cork is mature. The first stripping is done after some 25 years. In Portugal, this has been quantified to a minimum diameter of 80 cm (31.5 inches). The early growth of the cork tree is much like the early years of a varietal grapevine and the first harvest, the virgin oak, is irregular in size and density and not suitable for wine stoppers. Nine years will pass before the tree can be harvested again. The annual growth will range between 1.5 mm and 3.6 mm to produce a layer 26-28 mm thick. This second harvest and all following are called reproduction cork. A tree will yield 13 to 18 such harvests during its life.

Location

Special climatic needs restrict the cork oak's propagation to a rather small area — around the western Mediterranean Sea in lands influenced by the Atlantic Ocean. Here, there is relatively little rainfall, a great amount of sunlight, and a fairly high level of atmospheric humidity. There must be something else that is vital, something not yet identified, for all attempts to establish commercial cork groves elsewhere in the world have failed.

Portugal is the leading producer of cork, responsible for slightly more than half of the world's production while Spain produces a fifth and Algeria an eighth. Italy, Morocco, France, and Tunisia are responsible for the final sixth. Most of these countries have enacted legislation to protect their cork production. The trees must reach a specified diameter before they can be harvested and further harvests cannot take place until a specified interval — in Portugal, there must be a minimum of nine years between strippings — and the harvests must take place in specified periods during the year.

The density of production varies from country to country with the varying soils and climatic conditions. Portugal is not only the most favored with the largest area under cultivation, it also has the highest yield per hectare in cultivation. Morocco, immediately to the south, has a much lower yield, actually less than a fourth, and Spain, immediately to the east, has a little more than a half. There seems to be a delicate balance of factors that, so far, man has had very little success in controlling or altering.

A cork grove after the bark is harvested.

Evolution of the Cork Wine Closure

Cork has been a tool of man for six thousand years. It was used in the Egyptian Empire as early as 4,000 B.C. for fishing floats and buoys. Cork in any form always floats. Water will neither shrink it nor expand it, which again demonstrates the impermeability and elasticity of the material. By the time of the Greek and Roman periods of dominance, cork was being used as closures for amphores and casks. Pliny the Elder writes of it in Book XVI of Natural History, about 70 A.D., "...its only useful product is its bark, which is extremely thick and which when cut grows again; when flattened out it has been known to form a sheet as big as 10 feet square. This bark is used chiefly for ships' anchor drag-ropes and fishermen's drag-nets and for the bungs of casks....". But it was not until the late seventeenth century when cork began to be used to seal bottles that it achieved its position as a wine stopper. Until that time, wine was aged in large casks in the merchants' cellars or private cellars and brought to the table in pitchers or in bottles which were broad bottomed for stability.

Once the cork stopper became available, minds were stirred to bring about two developments — the mould for making cylindrical bottles and the corkscrew. Wine could not be aged in bottles as long as they remained bulbous. The bottle had to lie down to keep the cork moist. To produce a cylindrical bottle, which could lie down, uniform in size and shape, it was necessary to develop the glass mould. Secondly, there needed to be a practical method for removing the cork from the bottle and some anonymous genius invented the corkscrew. These developments were stimulated by the fact that there was a lot of Port in England at reasonable prices and it benefited

greatly from bottle aging.

Cork quickly achieved recognition and acceptance. Until the 20th century, virtually every bottle was closed with a cork stopper. This stimulated an increase in the cultivation of cork trees and the subsequent development of an organized industry. The increasing production of cork stoppers generated great quantities of scrap which led naturally to the search for and the development of new uses for the wasted material.

The answer lay in reshaping the odd forms of the waste by granulating the cork and then binding the granules into useful forms. This was done in two ways, producing agglomerate cork and composition cork. Agglomerate cork uses the material's natural resins to bind the granules together under heat and pressure. In composition cork, other binders or plasticisers are added to produce a range of materials with different properties. Composition cork is used extensively in the manufacture of sparkling wine closures, however the industry has adopted the term agglomerate when speaking of these closures and this book will conform to that usage.

The response to the growing demand for cork bottle stoppers and development of the other applications have produced a stable and efficient manufacturing process. By the late 1970's, there were some 500 industrial units in Portugal producing nearly twenty billion cork stoppers annually. Including those working in the cultivation and harvesting of bark, more than 50,000 people, out of a total population of three million, are occupied in the cork industry in Portugal.

Sorting and grading wine stoppers, Portugese factory.   19

Cultivation

Although the cork oak lives in a forest environment, it requires a significant amount of attention in order to achieve optimum production of quality bark. Periodic pruning is required to restore the balance of growth which is affected by the stripping of the bark. Pruning is also used to shape the tree to achieve the maximum production of cork and to facilitate its removal in large sheets.

It is widely believed that the use of chemical and other artificial ferilizers results in inferior cork quality. Extensive testing is currently underway in Portugal to determine the effects of fertilizing with varying soil nutrients.

The harvesting of the bark takes place during the summer months, from June to August. This is the maximum growth period with sap circulation at its peak. The stripping is done with a special axe. The metal head is used to cut the bark and the handle end is shaped to assist in detaching it carefully. As mentioned earlier, the cork trees are protected by government regulations specifying the growth which must take place before harvesting is allowed.

Once the cork is stripped from the tree, it is stacked in piles to aerate. Residual sap and moisture are removed in this open air storage which will last from three months to a full year. This is an important step, especially for cork to be used for stoppers. Defects, revealed by differential shrinkage during this drying period can be detected and the bark removed from stopper manufacturing.

In Portugal, the variation in drying time is also a factor in the geographical structure of the cork industry. Unlike the wine industry, the manufacturers of cork products are located some distance from the growing areas. Most of the

Stripping cork bark with specially shaped axe.

manufacturers are located in the north, near the city of Oporto, while the forests are in the south central region, east of Lisbon. A few of the manufacturers own trees and some of them are expanding their holdings but most of them send representatives to the south to purchase the bark. The bark is then transported to the north by truck regularly throughout the year. Increasingly, the initial manufacturing operations are done at the harvest location. Completing the boiling, drying and grading operations in the forest brings shipping economy and efficiency as the various grades can be trucked direct to their users.

When the cork is brought to the factory, the slabs are still curved in the shape of the tree and contain 15% or more of moisture. Many have small pockets of highly concentrated moisture. These are called "green". The cork is either stacked for further outdoor storage or baled for handling.

Each slab of cork, from one to two feet wide from the circumference of the tree and three to four feet long, is taken vertically from the trunk or major limbs of the tree. They are 26-28 mm thick, averaging 3 mm per year for nine years. The slabs are baled in blocks of a cubic meter or so for handling in the factory.

Harvested cork drying.

Manufacturing

The initial factory operation submerses the bales in boiling water for about an hour. With chemicals added, the boiling kills organisms in the bark and renders it more elastic and pliable and more amenable to flattening. Following the boiling, the slabs are flattened and stacked to dry. The drying period lasts about three weeks and during this time the bark develops a coating of white fungus on the outside or bark side. The inside, the side closest to the tree trunk , is called the "belly". The fungus forms on the third day and disappears several days later. This then signals that the cork is ready for further processing. At this stage, it is semi-rigid with a moisture content of 15 to 18%.

The cork slabs are then removed from the bales and graded. The separating into different thicknesses and qualities is a highly specialized task, the selection made in accordance with the suitability of the cork to a particular purpose. Only the highest quality is selected for stoppers.

During the selection, the edges of the slab are trimmed to yield a roughly rectangular piece approximately two feet by four feet. The slabs of appropriate thickness are then sliced across the grain to just over the desired stopper length. In factories with automatic punching machines, the slices may be graded for quality with the highest quality going to the automatic equipment.

The cork stopper is punched on a machine resembling a lathe with a rotating steel tube as the punching tool. On a manually operated machine, the operator advances the slice of cork by hand. He skips over defects while trying to keep the spaces between punches to a minimum. On an automatic machine, the slice of cork is fed and punched at uniform intervals with minimum spacing. The punched

Sterilizing and softening cork slabs.

Grading and trimming cork slabs.

Punching cork wine stoppers.

cork stoppers are ejected into a net bag and the "Swiss Cheese" remnant tossed into a basket for removal to a grinder. A punch operator produces 10,000-15,000 corks per day, one every few seconds. It is demanding work.

The punching process produces a rough cork stopper. Several finishing operations may be required, depending upon the application. First, the ends of the stopper are squared off by transporting them between parallel disc sanders. The stoppers are punched with tools that are a standard size. Odd sizes are made by sanding or trimming with a blade. Chamfering and tapering are done similarly. Stoppers for bar top or bulb top corks are chamfered for delivery to all markets. Straight wine corks are chamfered almost solely for the U.S. market and that is changing rapidly. Only a minority of U.S. wineries are still using chamfered straight corks.

When the shaping and surfacing is completed, the cork stoppers are loaded into net bags and bleached and washed. The bleach may have been natural or a rosé. Until recently, it was thought that there was no functional difference between the two, that it was just a matter of preference. However, recent reports of testing in Europe indicated deleterious properties contained in the rosé bleach and its use is no longer permitted in France and Germany.

The use of any bleach may be eliminated due to research carried out in Portugal in 1982 to ascertain the variables in the passage of wine between the cork and the neck of the bottle through capillary action. The testing was extensive, covering the absorption of wine in corks and the force of withdrawal of the stopper from the wine bottle. Several important conclusions were drawn from the resulting data:

    1. The use of abrasives to size corks has a negative effect

on the functioning of the cork stopper.
2. Clean water washing is preferable to any bleach.
3. If bleach is used, surface treatment is essential.
4. The amount of surface treatment is critical.

Following the washing and the rinse, the bags are spun dry. Once the surface moisture has been removed, the stoppers are placed on a conveyor and passed through a continuous drying oven or are vacuum dried which is more efficient particularly in rainy winter months. Only the surface pores are being dried. When punched, the moisture of the cork is 15+% and it is about 15% when it emerges from the drying oven.

Moisture content is very important to the actual bottling process and it should be a key quality control factor. All sizing operations of cork stoppers are performed at a moisture content in excess of 15%. Most U.S. customers receive stoppers at 6 to 10% moisture content. That is a guaranteed shrinkage of .010 inches. The relationship of moisture content to size of cork stopper is of obvious consequence if sizing is critical.

After the washing and drying, the stoppers are sorted or graded for quality. Most factories use seven grades, number one being the highest. The grading is done substantially by hand and is based principally on the number of voids on the surface of the stopper: the greater the number, the lower the grade. In Portugal, this work is done by women. Each cork is scanned individually and then tossed into the appropriate grade container.

A final inspection is performed using a roller conveyor to rotate the stoppers and move them quickly past the defects inspectors making visual checks. This operation picks out obvious defects within the given grade resulting in a higher uniformity of the grade.

The subject of cork stopper quality, grading and the

Cork stoppers are graded by visual inspection.

resultant cost is of principal interest to the buyer. This subject will be dealt with in detail in another section.

Another finishing operation, now declining in usage although it had been common practice, is the cleaning of the tops and bottoms with a sharp knife or disc. It is done to remove the lenticular channels which could drop some of the powder they contain into the wine. It is a slow hand operation and must be done with great care. Too many cuts or too deep cuts create additional edges which can become unstable in bottling and, by breaking, create a problem far more serious than the one the procedure was intended to solve.

The next operations prior to packing the cork stoppers for shipment are branding and surface treatment. Branding became a standard practice after the second world war. The practice arose in response to uncertainty about what really was in the bottle. The identifying brand on the cork stopper became the vintner-bottler's seal of authenticity and integrity. The mark is made by burning or printing on the cork stopper. Cork factories of any consequence can and do perform this function but more commonly today, the cork stoppers are shipped to their markets and the branding is done by distributors or the wineries themselves. Printing has become much more prevalent than burning and it is widely available in the United States.

Surface treatment is done to help to maintain the favorable characteristics of the cork and to provide protection against external contamination. Various processes are employed and special benefits are claimed and debated, however, the basic steps are dust removal and a surface treatment for coating or impregnating the cork.

Dust removal is simple and should always be perform-ed. The many processing steps in the manufacture of cork

Newly printed corks ready for surface treatment. 33

Tumbler units for surface treatment.

stoppers generate considerable cork dust. It must be removed or it will contaminate wine and, to be most effective, it should be done as near as possible to the place and time of usage. The manufacturers do not always perform this operation as a matter of course although they are capable. Some Portugese factories remove dust, surface treat and package the cork stoppers as well as they can or in ways they feel will protect their product. However, the long transit from Portugal to many countries, including the United States, generates additional cork dust and accumulates dirt. The local cork stopper distributor should remove cork dust and provide the winery with corks that are clean.

Surface treatment uses a material that will reduce permeability even further, reduce the coefficient of friction and resist the action of bacteria and fungi — to some degree. The most common process, by far, is simply coating the stoppers with paraffin wax. Paraffin exhibits all of the desired beneficial characteristics. In addition, it is simple and inexpensive and also has the weight of historical experience in its favor. The paraffin can be applied cold, warm, or in a liquid state. Its only drawback is that it can be overdone and then it is possible for chips or flakes to fall into the wine sometime after bottling.

Silicone is also used as a treatment agent and is applied in the same manner as paraffin and it can also be sprayed. The advocates of this material claim that silicone imparts greater lubricity and therefore eliminates many problems of stopper insertion.

A third category of treatment methods involves vacuum or pressure impregnation of the stoppers with one of a variety of proprietary chemicals and/or binders. In some cases, cork dust with a binder is impregnated into the stopper in an effort to reduce surface porosity. This

Cleaned, printed, and paraffined corks ready for packaging.   37

process is known as colmatage.

Packaging for shipment is done most commonly in plastic coated burlap bags or bales which will hold 12,500 corks. These have become somewhat the standard for handling, shipping, and protection. Another common package is a polyethylene bag which holds 1,000 stoppers. This package makes it possible to hermetically seal with the addition of SO_2 gas. The proponents of SO_2 claim that it is an effective bacteria-destroying and fungistatic agent. The addition of SO_2 is most often referred to as sterilization. Research conducted by the Wine Institute of Germany argues against SO_2 application. It found that sulfuric acid destroys the suberine and cellulose of the cork cell walls and causes stoppers to become hard and brittle in time.

However, commercial SO_2 cork sterilization was studied microbiologically in Australia in 1981 and the results were published in 1982. They clearly argued for SO_2 treatment since it was shown to be nearly 100% effective against molds and almost as effective against bacteria.

Cork stoppers are sterilized and sealed in plastic.   39

Sealing Wine

It may appear to be obvious that a well-made cork stopper needs to be properly sized and inserted with care if it is to do its work and seal the wine effectively as long as desirable. Yet the frequency of sealing problems in wine production indicates that subject merits some examination. While faulty cork stoppers may be responsible for some problems, the overwhelming number of instances that this writer has been asked to diagnose indicated faulty stopper specifications, variations in bottle configurations, or variations in the stopper insertions to be the cause. Each of these conditions deserves some attention.

The size of the cork stopper is critical. If the diameter is too small, the compression is inadequate for an effective seal and if the diameter is too large, wrinkles can form, also jeopardizing the seal. The stopper needs to be 6 mm larger than the interior diameter of the bottle neck for a still wine and 7 mm larger for a sparkling wine with gas up to 2.5 atmospheres. For the standard 18 mm neck and still wine, the cork stopper should be 24 mm in diameter.

For stoppers with bulb tops or bar tops (T-corks), the differential is much smaller — 2 to 3 mm. There, diameter control is critical. These stoppers are used for the larger containers and the aperitif and dessert wines; they are designed to allow the consumer to open the bottle by hand and to remove and replace the stopper many times. This lesser compression enables the winery to mechanically force the stopper into the bottle without requiring a machine to compress the cork to insert it.

The length of the cork depends upon the capacity of the bottle and the type of the wine. The 375 ml bottles are effectively sealed with a cork stopper 38 ml long, even with wines which require extended aging. A 38 mm

stopper can also work effectively with the 750 ml bottle for wines of relatively quick consumption. For wines that need to be laid down, a 44 mm stopper should be used. The 49 mm stopper has long been used for wines that are to be cellared a long time. Tradition and the assurance that the best possible stopper has been selected are probably the main reasons for its wide usage. In terms of the seal alone, it does not appear that a 49 mm cork stopper has any advantages over the 44 mm. But, in practice the results are perceived to be better. That, in the absence of scientific data, is good enough reason to use the longer stopper.

The ideal interior shape of the bottle neck is a perfect cylinder for the length of the sealing surface. This allows for easy cork entry and enables the cork to expand along its entire length to achieve maximum adhesion. Varying bottle configurations result in conical sealing surfaces and this produces smaller sealing areas. In extreme cases, this causes the cork to fall into the wine when pressed by a corkscrew. When this happens, the cause is the variation in the interior neck of the bottle and not the cork stopper.

The third problem area in achieving effective wine seals is in the cork inserting equipment. The system for compressing the corks must be in good condition and the piston that forces the cork into the bottle must be carefully centered. Inserting machines can damage the cork stoppers beyond their ability to recover and seal properly. Well-maintained equipment will eliminate this possibility.

Finally, it is recommended that the sealed bottles remain upright for 24 hours to allow the cork to recover from the compression it has undergone and to adhere fully to the walls of the bottle neck. To invert the bottles or lay them on their sides immediately after bottling increases the possibility of some wine penetrating between the cork

High speed bottling demands precision cork replacement.   43

and the glass and hindering adhesion. Studies have shown that cork recovers nearly 98% in two hours. The recommended 24 hours provide an added margin of safety.

As covered earlier, plastic top cork stoppers, known as bulb-tops, bar-tops, and T-corks have different requirements. Used in great quantities throughout the world, these stoppers are used to seal dessert, aperitif, and other sweet wines as well brandies and liquors. In recent years, these closures have become standard for sealing dry table wines in containers larger than 750 ml. They consist of a cork shank with the exposed end chamfered and the top bonded to a larger plastic ball or bulbous shape which works as a gripper or handle, enabling the consumer to open the bottle without a corkscrew and to easily reseal it, several times if necessary. Usually, these tops are engraved or otherwise decorated with the winery name or logo.

This resealing capability imposes special requirements in the manufacture of these corks. First, the size is more critical. The length must be sufficient to allow contact along the entire length of the glass sealing surface. The diameter must be precise since the cork cannot be compressed as much as the standard stopper. Instead of 6 mm machine compression, these stoppers cannot be compressed greater than 2 - 3 mm. If the diameter is too large, insertion and removal become difficult and, if too small, leakage will occur.

Secondly, the bonding is critical. The bonding agent must be compatible with food packaging. The majority of these stoppers produced in Europe are bonded with solvents which can, and often do, emit vapors which are trapped in the bag, box or other shipping container. These vapors can impart undesirable flavors to the cork and, therefore, to the wine.

Sealing Sparkling Wine

Sparkling wines provide an extreme test of cork's unique properties. Prior to insertion, a champagne cork is normally 30 mm in diameter and 50 mm in length. After insertion, the shank is reduced to about 20 mm and the head is compressed, reducing the overall length to 40 mm. This tortuous treatment is necessary to effect a seal of the bottle's pressurized contents.

Deformation of this sort requires the most unique material properties. The original sparkling wine stoppers were solid pieces of cork. Cost pressures led to bonding pieces together and 2-piece, 3-piece, 5-piece, and now 7-piece closures are the standard. This evolution required concurrent technical developments in the performance of adhesives and bonding agents.

The next step in the development of sparkling wine closures came from the technology developed for a wide range of cork products — gaskets, wall board, shoes, etc. This is agglomerate cork which comes from binding cork particles together. This process uses the scrap from the still wine stoppers, greatly increasing the usable yield from each cork tree and the larger sparkling wine closure was an ideal application for agglomerate cork. However, it is not a total blessing. The agglomerate cork sparkling wine stopper does present problems in quality control and, as a consequence, reliability can be questionable.

The requirements for a sparkling wine stopper are much the same as with still wine. The stopper must run in the bottling equipment, keep oxygen out, and be free of contaminants. The need to maintain the pressure of the sparkling wine in the bottle, however, generates a set of much more difficult requirements which can create problems with agglomerate cork. The agglomerate can:

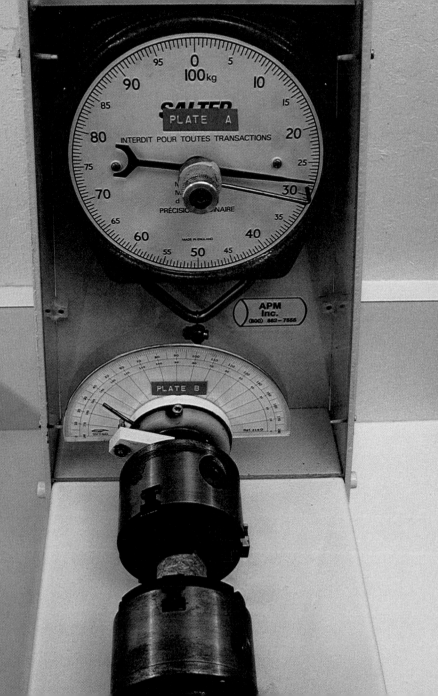

(1) be too hard to compress properly; (2) be of insufficient strength to withstand deformation and upon subsequent removal, break and crumble; and (3) harden after bottling thereby frustrating removal. These faults create havoc on bottling lines and total devastation with the consumer.

Why do champagne corks work some times and not others? What constitutes a good cork stopper? The answers to these questions lie in the manufacturing process and quality control. Many variables are involved: distribution of the cork granules and bonding agents, cork quality, density, humidity, the forming process — extrusion or molding, and the packaging, storage, etc. Several of the prominent sparkling wine producers in California are working diligently to establish specifications which will increase reliability of the stoppers. Excellent specifications are now in existence and mechanical tests are being performed. However, there is still a need to achieve a better understanding of the agglomerate microstructure and the factors which affect it. Then the process will move from art to science.

Alternatives to Cork for Sealing Still Wine

What choice does the winemaker have as an alternative to cork for the protection of still wine? There are several to be found in three different materials: agglomerate, metal, and plastic. All have significant limitations in application, performance, supply, cost or image.

Agglomerate As noted earlier, agglomerate suffers from variations in particle sizes, in density, and in the distribution of the cork particles and the binder. It cannot recover as fully from compression and effect the same seal achieved by a whole cork stopper. Still wines lack the tremendous upward pressure of sparkling wines which causes the mushroom shape of the stopper and forces the stopper to push out against the interior side of the bottle neck. Its greater rigidity and lesser flexibility also greatly increases the difficulty of removing the stopper. The consumer, armed with a corkscrew or cork puller, faces a formidable problem. It appears, however, that there may be good potential for the bulb and bar tops using agglomerate shanks. New binders appear to have overcome earlier problems.

Metal The simplest metal closure is the crown cap which has a liner and is crimped over the bottle lip. This "soda pop" closure is used in the methode champenoise and the transfer method of sparkling wine production. It is also used by some wineries for quick turnover sparkling wines. It is not capable of maintaining a seal for the life of a premium still wine and it poses handling problems, reducing its practicality for quick turnover still wines. On both functional and esthetic bases, the crown cap is not acceptable to the wine consumer.

Various aluminum screw caps are used extensively on "jug" wines. The roll-on, pilfer-proof cap has become an industry standard. The significant improvements in the design of the Stelvin style closure produced a reliable wine closure. Some wine industry people will argue that the sealing characteristics are superior to cork. However, this closure has a low quality, low price consumer image to such an extent that some producers cover it with a plastic overcap. Nonetheless, screw caps represent a significant portion of the lower price still wine market.

A third metal product is now finding a niche. This is the can as a container for quick turnover, especially in fast foods and airlines. There is no predictable application for the can as a container for premium still wines.

Plastic Plastic closures have been used for sparkling wines since the middle fifties. The closure design utilizes the internal pressure to assist and maintain the sealing. They function well and are acceptable for the high volume, fast turnover sparkling wines. They are not applicable to still wines at this time. However, some designs have been produced and are undergoing tests at several wineries.

In the last few years, a number of plastic products have been proffered as replacement for the cork wine stoppers. Generally, they have been made to look like cork and are either a foamed polyethylene or foamed ethylene-vinyl-acetate. A considerable amount of testing and promotion have been done but the sealing reliability, cost, supply and consumer image are all questionable.

A third area of plastic usage is the bag-in-the-box package. Both the bag and the valve are of plastic construction and the design is proving itself and gaining good acceptance. The package has found a niche in the institutional market and is bound to become the standard for the industry. Again, it is not applicable to premium still wines.

Cork Quality: Cork Cost
— the semantics of buying and selling

The discussion of cork quality versus price seems unending and it is age-old as indicated by this ancient Portugese parable:

An Appreciation of Cork

Cork is the overcoat of a tree which grows in the Western Mediterranean area.

It keeps the tree hot and cold, the grower broke and the buyer crazy.

Its texture, color, and density vary in different places, even from the same tree: and the man who guesses the sizes and qualities of the corks which can be cut from each piece is called a corkwood sorter (by the public), a thief (by the grower), and a numbskull (by the user).

The price of cork goes down after you bought it and up after you have sold.

Only superior quality is shipped, only rubbish is received.

These dilemmas which have been so emotion laden for so long are now yielding to the methods of science and reason combined with statistical methods. The problem is not imponderable. In simple terms, the winemaker wants assurance that his product will be protected for as long as necessary. Additionally, there is usually a desire for a very fine appearance. All elements of the package must reflect the image of excellence and the cosmetic qualities of the cork stopper are an important part of the consumer's experience with a wine.

Cork slabs dried, sterilized, and baled for shipment to factory.

These two aspects — function and cosmetic — need to be separated for purposes of analysis and discussion but this is not to imply that one is more or less important than the other.

Human judgment provides the basis for selection and grading of cork at every stage in the processing. With its limitations, the procedure appears to work quite well. Because these procedures are used for such enormous quantities, it is only through statistical methods that their effectiveness can be interpreted. The largest factories in Portugal produce 5 million corks per day and, despite great effort and care, some defective corks are bound to get through the visual inspection system. The sophisticated cork buyer attempts to minimize the problem by the use of statistically based specifications.

The major wineries in the United States have established comprehensive specifications in an effort to control the quality of the cork they purchase. The most sophisticated of these contain a general specification which covers the product. For example, one may state that the cork must be properly cured, aged, and processed; must conform to FDA regulations; must be neither too hard nor spongy; and must be free of excessive voids, dust, etc. All of this is an effort to arrive at some reasonable product definition.

A general specification will also include acceptance quality levels and sampling and inspection procedures. Sampling and inspection procedure plans normally conform to MIL-STD-105 and each winery applies its own AQL (acceptable quality level) to the various parameters.

How these items are classified or weighted will vary from one operation to another. A critical defect may be assigned an AQL in the range of 0.1 - 0.5% while a minor defect may have an AQL level of 5.0%.

Typical of AQL definitions are:

critical defects	major defects	minor defects
contamination	dimension variation	moisture content
failure to run in bottling line	voids, cracks, holes, chips	weight
	failure to adhere to grade	color
	coating flaws	packaging

Contamination is almost always considered a critical defect. It is the characteristic above all others that can adversely affect the wine. How contamination is measured and controlled varies widely but the usual indicators are appearance, odor, and taste of the wine. Sophisticated wineries immerse statistically selected samples of cork stoppers in the wine for 24 to 72 hours and then perform taste tests. The limitation in this is the difficulty of ascertaining whether the random sample is truly representative for that lot of stoppers.

This immersion test of random samples also indicates the excess of moisture content in the cork stoppers. Excessive moisture over an extended period will produce mold and a "corky" odor and taste. Until recently, moisture content was rarely considered as a major or critical quality criterion. It is, however, of extreme importance in the bottling application. Though the maximum water absorption of cork is only 18%, even small variations in water content can significantly alter the stopper's characteristics. The diameter will expand with added moisture and reduce with moisture depletion. The stopper can range from being very hard to very spongy. Either extreme can affect the compressibility during bottling and the integrity of the seal. Moisture content should,

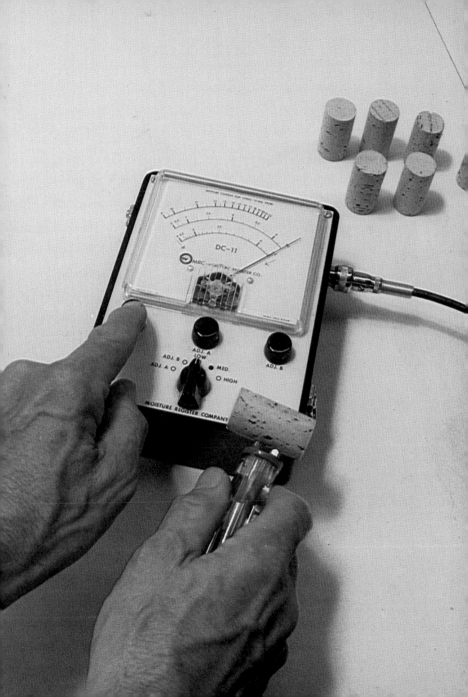

therefore, be considered as a key contributor to the critical defects list — contamination and bottling application.

Moisture content is most frequently measured with an electrical resistivity meter wherein two probes are inserted into the cork and the path between the probes indicates relative conductivity. While it is a relative measure, it is a reliable indication of moisture content. The acceptable moisture range for good cork stopper insertion is 6-10%. Moisture can and should be controlled as close to the actual time of use as possible.

The individual specification defines a specific item and covers: grade, dimension, weight, moisture, coating, compressibility, extraction force, chamfering, branding, and packaging. The corks received are then inspected according to sampling plans at specified AQL levels and the lot is accepted or rejected based upon the results.

This procedure works quite well and it can be greatly simplified and still be effective for smaller wineries. The main difficulty usually occurs in the definition of grade. The term is used both formally and informally throughout the industry. The Portugese producers use seven grades to define quality, generally designated by the numerals 1 to 7. The difficulty probably began when some creative soul began to designate the grades A to G. Now, throughout the world but most notably in the United States, there is a plethora of terms that have rendered the grading system almost useless. Who can know what "extra first" means? How does it compare to "first" or to "B" or to "super extra select"? The superlatives have become so inflated that one might think the cork business has been taken over by Madison Avenue.

The grading system is intended to exclude the defective corks to prevent damage to the wine but in practice, the system is concerned mostly with cosmetics. There are

reasons for this. The functional defects are few. Stoppers with substantial cracks, channels caused by overlapping punching, and large voids are usually eliminated in the visual inspections. This despite the fact that throughout the grading process in Portugal, no special attention is directed to these functional defects. Basically, cosmetic appearance is the criterion but it works out that specially selected cork stoppers based only on cosmetic appearance also will be almost entirely free of functional defects.

What is acceptable should be dictated by the application. A standard #9 cork stopper is compressed 25 to 30% when it is inserted into the bottle. Obviously, small voids and cracks are eliminated in the compression. Plastic top corks — bulb and T-corks — are normally compressed 10% or less and greater care must be applied to removing voids and cracks and to hold dimensional tolerances.

It is fair to assume that the Portugese cork stoppers producers would be happy to eliminate the grading process. If they could select cork wood, punch the stoppers, and ship the result at a fair price they would be very pleased. But the market dictates different quality standards, so they must respond. We can assume that the cost effectiveness of the extreme grades is fairly clear. A buyer of grade 7 takes what he gets at the lowest price and runs some risk that a high percentage of his bottles may leak. The buyer of grade 1 pays the highest price and has a high degree of confidence that his failure rate will be very low. It is when one steps down into these standard grades that the definitions become blurred.

What is the buyer of grade 3 or grade 4 thinking? Compromise! I'll lower my price and increase my risk. But it is natural for a buyer to want the best possible quality for the lowest possible price, so the game begins. The buyer says, in effect, "I want grade 1 but I'll only pay the

Microscopic examination of statistically selected sample.   59

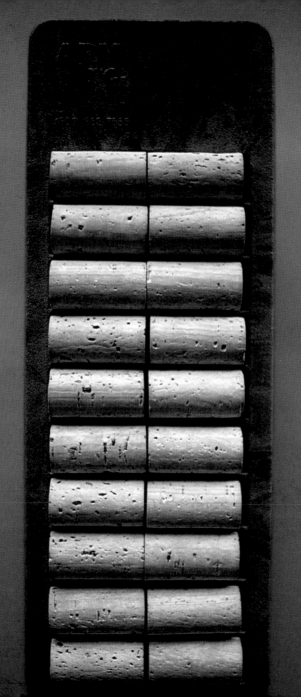

price of grade 3". The seller says, "O.K." But we all know there is no free lunch; the buyer pays for grade 3 and gets grade 3 but it's called grade 1. It is not very long before the buyer concludes that the seller's grade 1 is not good enough and his risk is too great. The seller says, "O.K., I'll give you Super Double Extra First but the price obviously will be higher". Now the buyer gets grade 1, but pays extra for it. The experience is a classic case of miscommunication.

The key for the buyer is to select the price-quality grade that suits his needs, insist on consistency, and buy from a reliable supplier. Within a given grade, there is a normal distribution of quality. Typically, within grade 2, about 60% of the lot will be grade 2, and 20% will be better and 20% will be a lower grade. The seller will alter the percentages or skew the distribution to fit what he perceives to be the buyer's situation.

It is apparent that the price-quality evaluation can become highly subjective. The array of terminology applied to the grading process does not help but the buyer and seller can take positive steps toward clarity of communication and reliablity of performance. The buyer sets the standard and along with the seller decides what it will be called. Library samples for comparison with lot samples should be established. The buyer should look at entire lots and take multiple samples to insure reliability of the sampling. Sample trays are used in Portugal to facilitate comparison with standards. They are simple but they do organize the comparison process.

Automated, computer-controlled sorting equipment is beginning to be used. These systems enable the user to pre-program the standard and then separate all stoppers falling short of that quality level. Two basic technologies

Sample tray used for visual comparisons.

are used — optical and pneumatic. The optical system looks at each cork and makes light-dark comparisons, rejecting excessive dark which signifies voids. The pneumatic system measures air flow across the cork surfaces. These methods have had their limitations but the systems are improving quite rapidly. They will certainly see greater use, if only to sort out and remove all of the unquestionably defective cork stoppers, however, it is also very likely that their discriminatory capacities will be greatly improved as further development takes place.

The price-quality uncertainties can be greatly reduced. Reasonable specifications, comprehensively worded or abbreviated, and insistence on conformance should lead to proper pricing. Cork is a relatively free market commodity. It responds to supply and demand pressures and there are many suppliers. There will be price movements in both directions, as history has demonstrated.

Conclusion

Despite continuing efforts to develop and establish acceptable substitutes, natural cork will remain the primary closure for wine for many years to come. The things that stimulate the search for an alternative — cost, consistency, reliability — have also stimulated the cork industry.

This centuries-old business is moving into the modern era at a rapid pace. The concern about long-term supply is unfounded. Reforestation is being expanded and the production is sufficient to accomodate considerable growth in United States wine production. The producers are applying automated technology and controls to their operations and it is reasonable for the American winemakers to demand that their suppliers keep pace. Cork is a natural, traditional and efficient closure with an extra-ordinary history and a bright future.

Bibliography

Magazines and Journals

Lee, T.H., Fleet, G.H., Davis, C.R. "Inactivation of Wine Cork Microflora by a Commercial SO_2 Treatment," *American Journal of Enology & Viticulture*, Vol.33.No.2. (1982)

Rubin, Hank. "Closures," *Wine*. June - July, 1980.

Pamphlets and Periodicals

Cork. Fundo De Fomento De Exportacas. Various pamphlets.

Cork - Naturally in the 20th century. Cork Industry Federation.

Cortica. Instituto Dos Produtos Florestais. Monthly magazine of the Portugese cork industry. Various.

L'art du liege. Centre Technique de Documentation du Liege.

Perez, Carlos. "The Cork Stopper, That Unfamiliar Thing," A series of articles in Portugese, source unknown.

A Note About The Book

The typeface is Baskerville, originally designed by John Baskerville in 1762. The composition was done by Casey Hobbs Design in Napa, California and the printing and binding is by the Kingsport Press in Kingsport, Tennessee. Photography of Portugese cork operations were provided by A. Paulo Amorim & Filhos, Lda., Rufino Alves Ribeiro & Filhos, and Sociedade Nortenha de Cortiças, Lda. The design and APM photography by Gene Dekovic.

Forty million cells per cubic centimeter, minute compartments of air, compressible and recoverable — this is cork.